AF658286

Evincepub Publishing

# Evincepub Publishing

Nehru Nagar, Bilaspur, Chhattisgarh 495001

First Published by Evincepub Publishing 2021



**ISBN:** 978-93-5446-304-4

To U.N.
WITH LOVE

# THE HOLY END

A WRITEN BY
SANIDHYA SHARMA

# ABOUT THE BOOK

The book is about creating the awareness about the change or reforms that we need today so that our so called efforts to save the environment that are going in somewhat diverted path from their goals, to the path of observation and taking right actions. What we need is that to focus on our activities that we do and what effects they cause to the environment.

The main idea is that if we want to improve the conditions of the environment, then the human beings have to observe and look their activities and try to improve the self, and hence the good effects can be seen in human beings as well as environment.

# ABOUT THE AUTHOR

The author loves to explore the logics behind the unique creations of the universe.

# What is U.N. (United Nations)?

In formal defination U.N. May be defined as an international intergovernmental organisation that aims to mantain international peace and security, develop friendly relations among nations, achieve international cooperation, and be a centre for harmonizing the actions of nations.

In simple terms U.N. Is simply an international organisation in which almost all the nations present In the world represent themselves under one roof, so that the maintainance of the world peace, protection of the human rights, and solving of any problem in any part of the world can be done equally by anyone and everyone, from around the world, is simply the U.N.

United nations is simply a platform, where the ideas can be expressed by anyone directly to the world leaders, so that the right idea may reach to the right people in right time, in right manner, with talks, discussion and representation.

When it comes to the enviornment, then U.N. Is having a good and old history, not much old but a good one.

Some of the famous agreements or reports by U.N. On climate change are:-

1.United Nations conference on the enviornment, 1972, Stolkholm.
2.United Nations framework convention on climate change (UNFCC), 1992.
3. United Nations conference on enviornment and development, Rio de Janeiro, Brazil, in 1992.
4.Kyoto protocol, 1997.
5.Paris agreement, 2015.

As there are many agreements, meetings and conventions which leads the countries to focus on the issue of the enviorrnment protection and to solve the raising problem of the climate change.

The policies by U.N. And the efforts by the countries had shown certain effects on the enviornment, but the remarkable feast that is required to solve the problem of climate change today is somewhere missing.

There are certain things which we need to understand and the change in our way so that we can understand the actual true position and how to solve the problem of climate change.

In the book I have described some of the ideas that are required and may help to tackle the problem of the climate change, and we should understand that it is the need of an hour to amend our policies if we want to solve the issue of the climate change.

The greatest undeniable law of nature is change, and change is the only constant thing. Throughout the long span of time period from formation of earth to the rise of life to the industrialisation many things had changed, and with change there comes the ways and processes that are also needed to change for the smooth functioning of the elements of the change.

The main idea here is that, from past few decades we tried some of the best things, stratigies and policies to protect the enviornment but now we should understand thet we can not protect or save the thing that has sheltered us and protected us for so many millions of years from many enviornmental dangers.

So what we can do?
Find out the answer in this book, which is a more likely a set of ideas, more than a book, towards tackling the problem of the climate change.

The U.N. Is a platform and I show my interest to express certain views, ideas and policies that can prove helpful towards understanding the environment and issue of the climate change, and right steps that we can take to tackle this problem of climate change.

The smoke not the air to breathe, the bacterias and germs not the water to drink, the chemical not the food to eat, the destructive brains not the building ideas. This is the reality of todays changing and so called modernisng and developing world. The develpoment of the world sits on the dead bodies of the innoscent creatures, the beautifull birds and the millions of the trees and the habitats of many animals. This is not the only thing but the human is the biggest enemy of human and between this rivalary the enviornment is the thing that is suffering the most and still we are calling it a development. The development of the nation is measured by the deadly weapons it have, but not by the natural beauty it possess. We are not sharing the love of the beauty with each other, but spreading the hate and ego between each other.

We have totally disturbed the balance of the nature in the name of so called development and we are becoming so much blind about the nature and the enviornment that we are not able to see the extent of damage we have done to the different components of the enviornment with long span of time. We should undersatnd that there is no planet-B, and if it's mars, then we have to think twice and think right with patience that till we will reach there it will be too late and only the few will be there who will make it and those few will also diminish in the space and there will be nothing left but only the sun and the planets surrounding it and the silence of the universe and space.

UNDERSTAND,
IT'S PAINFUL TEARS.

## THE HOLY END

# TABLE OF CONTENTS

## FICTIONAL PART



## THE FACTUAL PART

### SOME INTERESTING THINGS TO LEARN AND KNOW

# INTRODUCTION

WHO STARTED THIS, NOW PLEASE DON'T YOU
ASK,
WHO WAS THE FIRST AND WHO SHALL BE THE
LAST.

WHAT WE HAVE DONE TO THE NATURE
IS FAR THRETNING THEN FEAR.
STILL WE ARE NOT ABLE TO
WE THINK,
FALLING OF TREES IS JUST BECAUSE
OF THE WIND THAT PASSES BY,
BUT THIS IS NOT THE STORY MY FRIEND,
THIS THE PRICE BECAUSE OF HUMANS
THAT THESE TREES HAVE TO PAY.

SATNDING TALL FROM PLECETOCENE
AND SOME ARE FAR OLDER THAN THAT,
THROUGH MANY WINDS AND MANY STORMS
EVERYTHING FOR THEM WAS VERY GLAD.

NOW WHAT HAS HAPPNED TO THE STANDING
TALL PRIDE,
EVEN A SMALL FLOW OF WIND CAN MAKE
THEM FALL AND WIPE.
WE THINK,
OCEANS AND SEAS ARE PROUD OF THEM,
AND BY RAISING THIR HEAD THEY SPLASH

CITIES AND TOWNS,
BUT IT IS THEIR REQUESTING HAND
THAT THEY RAISE TO PRAY TO THE HUMANS,
AND THIS IS THE REALITY MY FRIEND.

WE THINK,
CLOUDS ARE NOT KIND BECAUSE THEY RAIN
RUTHLESSLY,
WE THINK SKY DON'T SHOW ANY MERCY,
BECAUSE SUN KEEPS IT HEAT CONTUNUSILLY
PIOERCING.

WE THINK,
THEY KEEP ON CHANGING THEIR GEAR
BUT THIS IS HOW THEY EXPRESS,
THEIR PAIN BY SHEDDING THEIR TEARS.

WHO STARTED THIS,
NOW PLEASE DON'T YOU ASK.
WHO WAS THE FIRST,
AND WHO SHALL BE THE LAST.

WELL SOMEHOW FROM A PEACEFUL DISTURBING SLEEP THROUGHOUT THE NIGHT I WOKE AND WASH MY FACE AND WITH TOWEL MY FACE I WIPE. I SAT DOWN FOR MEDITATION AND START LISTENNG MY PEACFUL FLOW OF BLOOD THROUGHT MY BODY, THE WINDS WERE FLOWING PECEFULLY AND THE CLIMATE WAS COLD AND CHILLY. THE VOICE I HEARD THAT

DAY OF THE THREE FRIENDS IT SEEM, WAS TOTALLY NEW FOR ME, THE TREE, THE SKY AND THE RIVER WERE TALKING ON THE TIME OF TEA. AS I LISTENED TO THE COVERSATIONS AND SIT PEACEFULLY SO THAT I CAN'T DISRUPT THEM, I THINK IT IS VERY JOYFUL EXPIRENCE AND I SHOULD NOT MISS THEM.
THIS IS THE INTRODUCTION WHAT THEY TALK IS SATRTED TO SEEM ME A BIT OF CREEPY, I BECOME COMPLETELY ACTIVE FROM THE STATE OF SLEEPY.

THOUGH ONE DAY IN MY ROOM
I WAS SITTING ON MY BED,
THEN SUDDENLY TO SOMETHING IMPORTANT,
MY ATTENTION LED.

I SEE THE TREE TOUCHING THE SKY,
THAT OUTSIDE MY ROOM'S WINDOW IT
RESIDES BY.

THE LEAVES WATCHING WITH HOPE
TOWARDS THE SKY.
HOPING FOR SOMETHING MIRACLE IN THEIR
LIFE,
HAPPEN BY.

I HEARD TALKING TREE AND SKY,
BOTH WERE TALKING ABOUT THE
RUTHLESSNESS,

BY HUMANS ON THEM LED BY.

THE TREE WAS THOUGH COUNTING THE SINS
OF HUMAN
ON HIM AND HIS FELLOWS,
COMPLAING AND PRAYING TO THE SKY
HOW WITH TIME ITS TRUNK IS BECOMING
HOLLOW.

I HEARD TREE REQUESTING AND PRAYING
WITH HOPE TO THE SKY.
PLEASE BRING ME TO YOU,
BECAUSE IF I WILL LIVE THEN I WILL DIE.

I HEARD TALKING TREE AND SKY MY FRIENDS,
I HEARD TALKING TREE AND SKY,
BOTH WERE TALKING AND COUNTING THE
RUTHLESSNESS OF HUMAN,
ON THEM BEING LED BY.

AFTER LISTENING TO THEIR TALK I UNDERSTAND THE MATTER, IT IS NOT THAT MUCH SMLL AND WE HAVE TO DO SOMETHING OTHERWISE LATE WILL BE VERY LATER AND QUICK ACTION WILL BE BETTER.
THOUGH WHAT TREE SAID I HEAR IT AND I GOT IT PROPERLY UNDERSATND, AND I THINK YOU SHOULD ALSO LISTEN THIS SO THAT WE CAN BETTER PLAN.

# “THE PRAY OF THE TREE TO THE SKY.”

O SKY PULL ME TO YOURSELF,
AND SETTLE ME IN THE MOON.
WHERE I CAN SLEEP FOREVER IN PEACE,
NO MATTER NIGHT OR NOON.

O SKY TAKE MY HIGHEST BRANCHES AS MY HAND
ASKING FOR HELP TO FLIGHT.
IT IS BECOMING HERE DIFFICULT WITH POLLUTION AND HUMAN BEINGS,
TO FIGHT.

O SKY I KNOW THE RAIN IS LIKE AN ACT OF KINDNESS,
THAT IS AGIFT FROM YOU.
BUT RAIN OF AXES ON OUR BRANCHES OF INSANE HUMAN BEINGS,
IS HOW THEY TREAT ON US RAĖMAING FEW.

O SKY PULL ME TO YOURSELF,
AND SETTLE ME IN THE MOON.
WHERE I CAN SLEEP FOREVER IN PEACE,
NO MATTER NIGHT OR NOON.
MY DAZZLING HEIGHT THE HUMANS THINK
IS LIKE A BEAUTY OR ENTERTAINMENT FOR THEM.

BUT I AM ASKING YOU O SKY
THIS IS ME ASKING FOR YOUR HELP.

THE LIFE I GAVE TO THE
INFANTS OF THE EARTH.
ARE FORGETTING THEIR BIRTH
AND LEADING TOWARDS MY AND THEIR
DEATH.

O SKY TAKE MY HIGHEST BRANCHES IF
POSSIBLE
AS MY HAND ASKING FOR HELP TO FLIGHT.
IT IS BECOMING HERE DIFFICULT WITH
POLLUTION AND HUMAN BEINGS
TO FIGHT.

O LORD, O GOD, O UNIVERSE
WAHTEVER YOU ARE CALLED,
PULL ME WITH YOUR MIGHTY FORCE, IT WILL
PAIN I KNOW,
BUT I AM NOW BOLD.

O SKY PULL ME TO YOURSELF
AND SETTLE ME IN THE MOON,
WHERE I CAN SLEEP FOREVER IN PEACE,
NO MATTER NIGHT OR NOON.

I KNOW, I WILL NOT ABLE TO DANCE THERE
BY MOVING MY LEAVES.
BUT MORE THAN A DANCE, I WILL SLEEP DEEP

AND THIS I WHAT NOW MAKES ME PLEASE.

MY LEAVES WILL FALL AND MY BODY WILL
SHATTER
ON THE MOON I KNOW
BUT IT WILL BE GOOD TO SLEEP PEACEFULLY
IN YOUR LAP O MIGHTY
THAN TO DIE EVERY MINUITE LIVING HERE
WITH HUMANS AXES AND BOW.

THERE WILL BE NO LAND ON MOON OF
HUMANS,
THAT THEY WILL SAY I OCCUPIED.
I WILL SLEEP THERE FOR EVER IN PEACE,
AND NOT FOR ONLY WHILE.

O SKY LISTEN AND GRANT MY WORTHY PRAY
AND PULL ME TO YOURSELF AND SETTLE ME
IN THE MOON.
WHERE I CAN SLEEP FOREVER IN PEACE,
NO MATTER NIGHT OR NOON.

O LORD, O SKY, O ALMIGHTY PULL ME TO THE
MOON.

JUST LISTENING TO THE TREE MY TAERS COME OUT FROM THE EYES I DID NOT THINK OF THIS THAT THEY ARE PLANNING TO SAY EARTH A GOOD BYE.

"TO CHOOSE TO DIE WITH HONOR
IS A GREAT OPTION,
THAN TO DIE EVRYDAY ON EARTH ALIVE."
-THE TREE.

THE TEARS WERE JUST GIOING TO FLOW OUTSIDE OF THE EYES BUT THE SKY AT THE TREE REPLIED. FULL OF SORROW THE SKY SAID TO THE TREE, IN BRIEF IF FIRST I TELL YOU THEN IT SAID DON'T WORRY MY FRIEND WHEN END WILL BE NEAR WE BOTH WILL BE FREE.

# "THE MIGHTY SKY REPLIED TO THE TREES."

O MY FRIEND, O MY CHILD,
DONT SAY ME LORD FOR SAKE.
YOU ARE PRAYINBG WITH YOUR HEART AND TEARS,
THOUGH I AM NOT ABLE TO SAVE.

WHAT I CAN DO TELL ME MY FRIEND
THE SMOG IS MAKING VIEW BLIND.
HOW I PROVE TO YOU,
MY ACT OF KIND.

SOME PLACES IT LAST FOR DAYS
AND SOME WHERE FOR MONTHS IT STAYS.
I AM ABLE TO LISTEN YOUR PRAY
AND IN RESPONSE THERE ARE ONLY LOVING WORDS TO SAY.

O MY FRIEND, O MY CHILD, DONT
SAY ME LORD FOR SAKE.
I AM NOT IN THAT POSITION FOR YOU,
FOR THIS HONOR TO TAKE.

I WISH I COULD HUG YOU NOW,
THEN OR LATER OF REELIEF.
BUT TELL ME, IAM NOT ABLE TO SEE YOU AND
FOUND MYSELF IN THIS POLLUTION

DUST AND SMOG IF,
I TELL YOU IN BRIEF.

WHAT I CAN DO TELL ME MY FRIEND
THESE HUMANS HAVE MAKE ME BLIND LIKE
THEM.
ALL THE POLLUTION SMOG AND SMOKE,
ALSO MAKING ME SLOWLY AND GRADUALLY
CHOKE.

I WISH AND WANT TO HOLD YOUR HAND,
BUT NOT ABLE TO FIND YOU ANYWHERE.
AND I AM AFRAID THAT THIS CONVERSATION IS
NOT LAST
AND NOT ABLE TO SEE YOU FOREVER AGAIN.

O MY FRIEND, O MY CHILD, WE WILL GO TO
THE MOON
AND I WILL TAKE YOU WITH ME I SWEAR.
BECAUSE IF ONE WILL END THEN OTHER ALSO
HAVE TO
AND ON EARTH THERE WILL NOTHING LEFT
THERE.

O MY FRIEND, O MY CHILD,
DON'T SAY ME LORD FOR SAKE.
YOU ARE PRAYING WITHYOUR HEAT AND
TEARS,
THOUGH I AM NOT ABLE YOU TO SAVE.

What I can DO TELL ME ,Y FRIEND,
THE SMOG IS MAKING THE VIEW BLIND.
HOW I PROVE TO YOUY
AND SHOW MY ACT OF KIND?

DO NOT YOU BWORRY THOUGH NMY FRIEND
I WILL NOT LEAVE YOU AND WE WILL
GO TO the MOON TOGATHER ONE DAY.

"HUMANS THINK THAT THE RESULT OF THEIR
POLLUTION
BEING CRAETED WILL BE SEEN IN
DESTRUCTION OF
ONLY ONE THING OR ONE ASPECT OF THE
ENVIORNMENT,
BUT THEY ARE TOO MUCH WRONG FOR THIS.
WHEN THERE WILL BE THE END OF ONE
THERE WILL BE END OF HUMANS AND WHEN
THERE WILL ABSOLUTE END OF ONE THERE
WILL BE ABSOLUTE END OF LIFE"

- THE SKY.

AS I LISTENED TO THE SOUND OF CRYING CLOUD, TOWARD THE TERSS, THE FLOW OF TEARS WAS NATURAL FLOWING AS I WAS LISTENING TO THEM IN VERY PEACE.
IT WAS LIKE FISH OUTSIDE THE WATER WANT TO GO INSIDE THE WATER NEXT TO IT,
BUT EVEN AFTER JUMPING AND MAKING SOUND EFFORTS IT COULD NOT MAKE IT.

THOUGH THE SOUND OF WATER SPLSHING SUDDENLY COMES OUT, ASKING IN HOPEFUL MANNER TO THE SKY AND TREE I ALSO WANT TO GO TO THE MOON WITHOIUT ANY DOUBT. IN A VERY SWEET AND GENTLE BUT IN GRIEF THE SEA WAS IN AT THAT TIME, COUNTING ALL THE DEPLETION OF THE RESOURCES BY HUMANS AND THE DETRUCTION BEING DONE ON THEM.

# "THE WISH OF THE SEA."

O MY FRIEND, O MY DEAR I LISTEN TO NYOUR
TALK
AND IT MADE ME FULL OF TEARS.
BUT THE RISING WATER IN ME
THE HUMANS THINK IS JUST MELTING OF
GLACIERS.

YOU BELIVE IT OR NOT,
YOU WANT IT OR NOT MY FRIEND
I WILL ALSO COME WITH YOU AND HAVE TO
WHEN THERE WILL BE ABSOLUTE END.

NO RAIN FROM THE SKY,
ONLY BPLASTIC FROM THE LAND.
THIS HAS MADE HUMANS COMPLETELY MAD,
AND ARE LEADING TOWARDS THEIR END.

I AM ACQUIRING THEIR DISGUSTING CITIES
AND TOWNS THEY SAY.
BUT THE FOSSILS THEY BURNMAKING
TEMPRATURE RISE AND MELTING GLACIESR
THEN THERE IS NIOTHING TO DO BUT ONLY TO
SAY.

THE PLASCTIC AND WASTE OF THE HUMANS
THAT THEY THROW
STRIKE LIKE A BULLET TO MY CHEST.

ALL THE CREATURES AND LIFE IN ME,
ARE SLOWLY BECOMING DEAD.

NOW YOU BELIEVE OR NOT,
YOUWANT IT OR NOT MY friend.
I WILL ALSO COME WITH YOU,
WHEN THERE WILL BE ABSOLUTE END.

NO RAIN FROM THE SKY
ONLY PLASTICS FROM THE LAND,
THIS HAS MADE HUMANS COMPLETELY MAS,
AND ARE CLADING TOWARDS THEIR END.

THOUGH WE WILL PEACEFULLY SETTLE AND
SLEEP FOREVER I THE MOON.

"THE HUMANS ARE MAKING THEIR
OWN WAY TOWRDS THEIR AND THE END OF
EARTH
BELIEVE ME THERE IS NO ONE ELSE TO DO
THIS."

- THE SEA.

THE TEARS WERE NOT STOPPING FOR A MINUTE AS I WAS WATCHING THE TOP MOST LEAVES OF THE TREE, HOW IT WAS ASKING FOR THE HELP FOR THE SKY AS MUCH IT CAN SEEK.
THOUGH NOT THE SKY WAS IN POSTION TO HELP THE TREE, I GUESS IT WAS ALSO THIINKING TO MAKE THE TREES FROM EARTH

FREE.
SEA WAS WITHOUT ANY DOUBT WAS RAEDY TO GO TO THE MOON, NOW I WAS THINKING THEN WHRE WILL GO THE INSANE HUMAN.

THOUGH MY TEARS COME BY
DON'T KNOW OUT OF LOVE OR WRATH.
NOT TOWARD THE NATURE,
BUT TOWARDS THE HUMANS WRATH.

IT WILL NOT AFFECT THE NATURE
OR THE THREE FRIENDS ALONE,
BUT ILL HEALTH OF ANYONE OF THE THREE FRIENDS,
WILL TAKE UP EVERY ONE END AS A WHOLE.

THEY ARE TALKING AND KEEP ON TALKING ABOUT THEIR END.
NOW WE THE HUMANS HAVE TO THINK HOW THIS SITUATION WE CAN BEND.

IF NOT IN TIME
WE WILL BE ABLE TO MAKE THE NECESSARY AMEND.
THEN THERE WILL BE ONE THING ONLY,
AND THAT WILL BE HOLY END.

# THE JUDGEMENT DAY

The clouds were shouting and the lighting was pounding, piercing the clouds down to the earth it was continuesly striking. Nature's business now with humans was compltely done. The sea was not in peace nor thy the trees, the winds were also furious and from now there will be no sign of breeze.

The birds were shouting no chirping was there in the morning, every human was afraid what today the nature with them is doing. The tree started to sing the song of the moon, the cloud was happy and saying the drem will come true soon. The sea thy there bouncing happily, all the three friends now were there dancing peacefully.

"The Situation of Earth that day."

the burds I see were not in good mood,
and no sign of the chirping was ther,
the black clouds and dense fog
was visible everywhere.

Nor the samll cubs were playing in the jungle,
oh sorry!, the jungle was just in the books that time,
the beautiful craeture that we used to see,
were completely diminished by the humans crime.

Volcanos were blasting that depicts the thirst for
destrucyion,

beaware humas now its your time to pay the price
said the earth trembling and shakinbg,
now the earth started to act for the nature's rights.

The sounds of the humans were not louder than the thunder
that hit the earthg with the might,
evberyone ran for the shelter,
but eath was the only shelter that was suitable and right.

How they ran in a great hurdle
was the view to worth watchng said the nature,
remebring the huntinjg of the animals, and cutting of the forests,
that the humans call the adventure.

After some time the planet was warm and hot
and the peace was there for some time again
no land no water no humans no trees nor any creatures
were left to for the life on the earth to sustain.

Now the real joy of peace
and the sounds of thgunder were like sweet breeze
completely hot and beautifully red
this is how the earth to the human beings the lesson it preach.

There is now the real beuty
and nothing left to mend,
this is how the time will come
when there will be the HOLY END.

# THE FACTUAL PART
# SOME INTERESTING THINGS TO LEARN AND KNOW

What is there that we don't know today, what is right that we are not able to do today, why are we just still making the so called policies and not implementing today. The change will not come if we keep on making the policies, but we have to implement them and before we make any policies first do their practical by themselves whoever is there with there new ideas and set first an example towards that policy or idea and show the world practically how it is beneficial for human beings and enviornment too. If we take an examle then we can say that when teenagers raech to the stage when they are fully aurthorised to buy any vehicle and drive it, then, what we can do in this point is that simply take or buy any non polluting means like electric cycles, electric cars, or simply cycles.

But this is not going to work for the thrill? Well then there will be thrill when there will be no space to run and when the nature will say now enjoy this thrill. We need to undersatnd whatever we are doing, are doing for ourselves not for the so called showy thrill. The real adventure is that when we fulfill our duty towards the protection of the enviornment and this is what makes us real proud and a real hero to atleast contribute our part to protect the enviornment. This is a thing to undersatnd to all the youth, that whatever actions we will take today it will really going to affect the future of the world and if we will make the right choice today then our next generation will also think in right way and always opt for the right things and may innovate new things towards the protection of the enviornment and it may change whole of the situation after few genearations and the civilisations will be in sync with the nature again with peace, love and harmony. This is known as wave of change or simply a revolution, and this is a  need of an hour. It may if we want to.

IF NOT NOW,THEN WHEN
IF NOT WE, THEN WHO
IF NOT HERE, THEN WHERE.

# TREES: THE ANCESTORS OF THE LIFE ON EARTH

We cannot ignore the fact that how important the green life on this planet earth to support the other forms of the life on the planet earth. Yes we can say that before the life started on the planet earth of these trees, there were many forms of life on this planet, like microbes, worms, and many forms of aquatic and unicellular life.

How can we say that the trees forms the basis of life? But let me ask you a question, that, before there were no trees and green life on this planet earth, then, were we as a human beings and any othere complex life was present? Were we able to live in the volcanic enviornmrnt full of gases, chemicals and microbes and also boliling hot with variations in weather conditions even for an hour or more precisely for few seconds? Were these microbes were there to support you and any other complex life forms? Well it's simply no. yes, many will argue with a lots of scientific facts and other chaos, but let me tell you, just think a bit logically and let's think seriously to the concept first that I am trying to put forward. Who knows clearly what happened that time how the complex organisms formed and other chaos. But the thing is that when green life started to flouirush many complex life started to form amd many multicellular organisms started to ecolve with the span of time.

The start and growth of green life was the elixer of life for the majority of the creatures on the planet earth, and till time today only the green life is the elixer of life for the human beings and other creatures that are living on the planet earth.

Well what we are today doing to the elixer of our life? Just spliting and exploiting it! Just thinking over it and ignoring every aspect of their benefit towards our existence!

Well if I say this thing or not, this is true, that, "there will be no life possible on this planet earth if there will be no trees and other natural resources on this planet earth." just keep it simple and keep it clear.

Interestuing facts about the trees and other forms of green life on the planet earth.

1.) What we need is right direction and trees can also help us a little in this:

    The trees can help us find right direction if we are lost in the jungle or any other unknown areas where forest is present on the planet earth. The effects of the temprature, climate, weather and certain natural factors like daily sun rays pattern on the area on which the tree grows affects the physical features of the trees and we can see these features clearly on their different parts mostly on their trunk and bark.

    If we take an example, then, in northrern temprate climates, moss will grow on the northeren side of the tree trunk, where there is more shade. Also, a tree's rings can help point you in the right direction too. If you are in the northeren hemisphere, you can see the rings of the tree grow slightly thicker on the southeren side since it recieves more light. In the southeren hemisphere, the opposite is true, with rings being thicker on the north side.

Well, a little direction can help us to save our natural compass of survival in dificult situations.

2.) The trees are the longest, biggest, thickest living organisms on the planet earth:

well is it an elephant or whale or earlier existed dianosors that are counted among the most giant organisms ever found on earth?
Well my friends don't think so small upto this only, see a bit higher and further and think a bit big, the most huge, enormous and giant living craetures are presnt on this planet are trees. Well how can we see them, we just ignore them and we never counted them as living because we cut them we destroy them and we kill them. But the true thing is that, the trees are the biggest living craeture on this planet earth.

Giant Aspen tree is the biggest living organism on the planet earth. In utah, in north America, there is a clinal colony of an indivisual malequaking aspen determined to be a single living organism by identical genetic markers and assumed to have one massive

underground root system. It is also known as pando and the trembling giant.
It's specific name is: *Popolus tremuloides.*

How it grows?
The main reason for it's enomorous growth is its ability to clone in hundreds to thousands of numbers in a same set of saplings. The indivisual trunk of tree is having life span of approximately 130 years, as when the life of this earlier grown tree comes to its end the other one is reday as a young tree trunk and it further grows its roots and more saplings from the one single underground growing root arises and this is how in rhythemic cylcle this giant beauty keeps on growing.

Although it's life is in danger due to many human activities. Researchers from many universities, Utah State University among many universitues, found that this living giant beauty is dying slowly and one day it will completely diminish. 47,000 genetically identified clone trunks, all grow from enormous root system. The weight of the pando is estimated as, 6 million kg.
The trunks of the Aspen keeps on falling on the natural basis according to a particular cycle, so the age of the tree that is estimated bu scientists is based on the rate of the spread of the Aspen tree i.e. Pando. The age of Pando is estimated about 80,000 to 1 million years.

Each indivisual tree trunk lives for 130 years. Spread over 106 acers of land.

The pandos has survived the thousands of years with the changing climate, dazzling sunshine, winds and storms, rain and snowfall, but it may not survive us.

One of the shocking reason for it's declining rate of survival is the grazing of the native hervivore animals of the area. As we have hunted down the carnivore species upto very high numbers in that area that there is no control over the herbivore species population and they generally used to eat the grass, and new growing plant saples that are also small and part of the grass while they are in growing stage as saples, they also feed on them from the ground and this threatens the continuity of the beautuiul giant on this planet earth.

It's death will be the reflection of the cruelity of the human beings and it will show that upto what extent we have damaged the enviornment and disturbed its balance.

It is our duty to preserve this giant beauty and also all forms of green life present on this planet Earth.

3.) Trees can help us reduce strees:

There is not much to write and tell about this as you suerly have feel the pleasusre and relxation while walking across the green corridor, wheather it's the jungle, terkking or a small walk around the city side roads where tress are planted on both the side.

The greenery makes us feel happy. If we undersatnd it scientifically, then, trees releases a chemical called phytoncides when we breathe them in, it can reduce blood preassure, lower anxiety levels, and increase pain threshold.

So just have a little walk in greenery, it will suerly made you love with yourselsf and nature.

some other interesting green friends on earth.

**The largest**

1.) The General Sherman Tree:-

The Genaral Sherman Tree is the largest living tree in the world by volume at 52,508 cubic feet (1,487 cubic meters).
The scientific name of the tree is, S*equoidendron giganteum.* It is located in the Giant Forest of Sequoia National Park in Tulare County, in the U.S. State of California.

It's age is estimated to be 2,300 to 2,700 years old. But the story does not ends here.

There was the friend of general shrerman tree, which was murdered by human beings in 1940's, and is estimated to be 15% to 25% larger than the general sherman tree by volume.

There was one more tree larger than these and it was the Lindsy Creek tree with more than 90,000 cubic feet (2,500 cubic meters) was reported felled by a storm in 1905.

## The Tallest

Hyperion as the name suggests something different and extereme and special is a tree which is the tallest tree in the world.

It's height is measured at 115.85 m (380.1 ft.), which ranks it as the world's tallest living tree. The age of hyperion is estimated to be 600 years old according to Sillett, while other reports estimate it to be roughly 700 to 800 years old.

The park in which hyperion is located, there exists the world's second and third tallest trees named Helios and Lacarus, respectively.

## The Widest

The widest tree in the world is, Montezuma cypress, “el Arbol del Tule.”

it is located in Oaxaca, Mexico.

According to the measurement done on 2005, it's trunk had a circumfrence of 42.0m (137.8 ft). The age of tree is unknown, with estimates ranging between 1,200 and 3,000 years, and even one claim of 6,000 years. The best scientific estimate based on growth rates is 1,433 to 1,600 years.

This tree is also known as, "the tree of life."
Although this tree is having some story to tell, that, it is also slowly dying.
In 1990, it was reported that the tree is slowly dying because it's roots have been damaged by water shortage, pollution, and traffic, with 8,000 cars travelling daily on a nearby highway.

As we can see now that, the giant beauties of our world that is our green life is getting harmed by us and by our activities in many ways. It is our duty to protect them, and if we can not protect them, atleast we must not harm them. How these green lives are dying after the invasion of human species. The facts are that these tall giant beauties, which are standing tall and proud from centuries and even more than thousands of years, facing many storms and many extreme enviornmental changes, but as the activities of humans started to so called develop and humans become ignorant towards there doings then there actually the problem lies. The ignorance is the main problem, and one who really thinks about it then he or she must come with some practical solutions.
Though there is one thing, "always try."
The Earth is our planet and Earth is with water and trees and a cool breeze of air, and rest are just existence. Save trees and let them live.

# THE SEA: WHERE THE LIFE FLOWS.

The thing that almost we all know that the first form of life that is the ancestor of the present life on the planet Earth first emerged inside the water that is our sea or oceans. Yes!, this is not also true as science do not fully back this idea or theory but, till now theorotically as well as experimentally this is the most widely accepted idea about the origin of the life on the earth.

Well after the air pollution, water pollution is the biggest pollution concern in the world that is leading to the depletion of the fresh drinking water resources and leading towards the incresed sea level collectively due to the climate change due to the contribution of every kind of the pollution that is rising in the world.

One the biggest example of the depletion of the fresh water body is Aral sea, I think you might have heard about it. It began shrinking in the 1960's and had largely dried up by the 2010's.
The most surprising thing is that, when you will google about Aral sea, then it defines the lake as, "the Aral sea was an endorheic lake lying between kazakhstan in the North and Uzbekistan in the South."

Did you notice the surprising element? Well it is written the Aral "WAS" a sea, but "IS" not a sea. Wow!, so beautiful, right? You are so lucky to see the live example of the destruction of the lake, which was so huge as said to be sea, is now really had become like a lake and soon it will be like a desert instaed of the lake, if the effect of climate change will reamin to be continued in such an alarming speed. And the beautiful thing here is that, we are not taking the isuue of the climate change as alarming, but still thinking, it is just a new and fresh raising issue, and we are relax and listening more about climate change, shouting about climate change, painting about climate change and doing not doing that is needed to be done for the climate change.

Oh well there is a tradition of the competetions among the kids in the school and most heated topic is the climate change, wheather children have to paint on the climate change or pollution or the similar stuff like this, that affects or is affecting our planet, there are slogan writing competetions, poem and speech competetion, and when you grow a little then there is a debate or shouting competetion in the names of rallies, that really contributes for the noise pollution, I think. Ironical, huh? Well a bit truth is good to listen sometimes.

I don't know how many children get rerally affected or care to do something for enviornment, but what they really care about is the first prize. Well I can say this because I have really participated in these kinds of competetions, and these are competetions, that is why the actual output is like nil for the sake of enviornment, and to make children aware about the envirnment and the dangers it is facing.

I am not criticizing these things, but just expressing the reality that I had observed, and yes, I might be wrong, but atleast see and observe this thing with heart, and then you will realise this problem.

So what shuld be done instaed of these competetions is that, make every child sit in a school, and let any enviornment activist let them know about the real truths and condition of the earth equally and without the preassure of any competetion. As at that time he or she will be teaching some valuable lessons to the youth and if the regular classes, will be organised in all the schools for small children and a bit more craetively with the high school and collage students then, it will really open up the brains of the new generation towards the actual condition of the earth, and instaed of telling others, they will try to improve their habits that can actually save the enviormrnt faster then to juyt wasting our and others time to teach them abou0t the so called environment protection. Iam asking you, how can you protect the enviornment or nature or earth, as the things that have protected you from billions of years? No you can not, but what you can do is that just inculcate in yourself some humane characters that we have lost over passage of time, and have hurt our planet earth.

So, the main point here is that, “it's all on you, not others. Take good and right steps first, and then you will see the positive change around your enviornment and it can and will influence others to change their behaviour to the good and right, and hence the improvement from enviornment to nature and finally to the earth will take place. It is all about you."

Oh! we are talking about sea, and we just get so deep in the one concept, but I think we found the right thing, is'nt it?

Now let us explore the deep sea.

The one of the most common thing that we all know, is that, the oceans on the Earth covers more than 70% of the area, yes, we can also consider ocean as water.

1.) One of the most interesting things about the oceans is that, according to the ocean service, man has explored less than five per cent of Earth's oceans. As researchers strive to discover more we are continually getting to know our oceans better.
    Well, the ironical thing here is that, earlier the researchers did not explore the complete deapths of the oceans and other water bodies, and now that with the help of technology they are exploring it, then, they are finding intersting things like plastic to the farthest parts of the water bodies, even in the mariana trench.
    Now, if the furthrer studies will be contiunued with passage of time, then, the possibilities are like that, the researchers will find the dry rivers and the places

where lakes were used to be, but then they will be diminshed, and in the oceans instead of the beautiful creatures, they will find the plastic and debris.

2.) World oceans water or simply water on the Earth, produces more than 70% of the planet's oxygen.
The studies shows that marine plantation produces large amount of oxygen per meter cubic area than the land plants. The best examples of these types of the plants are algae, and phytoplanktons.
Well it tells us that there is vibrant and very alive life inside the water of our planet Earth.

3.) It is possible to find rivers and lakes beneath the ocean.
Well yes, it is an interesting thing and also a bit science but not a rocket science. When there is a change in the density of the water inside the sea or an ocean then due to the change in the density inside the ocean hence the lake or a river like composition can be seen inside th oceans or sea. The types of lakes inside the oceans or deep seas are known as brine pool.

4.) The deepest part on the earth is the mariana trench. It is approximately 36,200 feet deep. It is present beneath the Westeren Pacific ocean , in the southeren end of the Mariana trench which runs several hundered southwest of the U.S. Terretorial island of Guam.

5.) Well it is not the fact but yes, the water do not provoid us any calories or organic nutrients, but still it is the most valuable and vital for all forms of life. Yes, the beer is cool and chilled, but beer do not quench thirst, it is the water. On this Earth there is nothing that can take place of the water for its vital purpose and the way it suppoorts the all forms of life.

It is not only about to know the facts, but to understand the importance of water, and there is one reason enough to wake up to save water, and that is you. If there will be no water to drink then there will be no you, and there will be no life, that is supported by water, and almost all the life forms need water to live. Even fish drinks water.

"Water water everywhere, but not a drop to drink" , the lines quoted from the poem, "The rime of the ancient mariner", written by Samuel Tylor Coleridge. The line is being said by a sailor who is surround by salt water that he cannot drink.

"It is life, I think, to watch
the water. A man can learn
so many things."

-Nicholas Sparks,
The Notebook.

Save water, save planet, save life, but remember, it all starts with you. Dare to take right step.

# THE SKY: THE NEVER ENDING BEAUTY

what is sky? Is it the clouds or blue or red or black colour or is it just the universe we are looking at?

Yes, it will not be wrong if we say that sky is just the universe, and we just look at the infinite universe when we look at the sky.

But the problem is that there are ,many places where the univese is hidden due to the coverings of the pollution and that sheath makes the look at the universe a bit hazy and sometimes completely opaque.

Sky is infinite so there is no problem to that, but what comes between the sky and ground is the atmosophere of the planet which make the planet habitable. And if that atmosphere is covered by any of the pollutants then it really cover the sky with the thick or thin sheath of the pollution which then leads to the rise in temprature of the planet and hence give rise to the global warming.

The sweet concept of green house effects come into the play here.

What is green house effect?
According to the defination of the green house effect it is simply the natural process that warms the Earth's surface.

When the sun's energy reaches the Earth's atmosphere, some of it is absorbed and radiated by greenhouse gases. The absorbed energy warms the atmosphere and the surface of the Earth.

The green house effect is good thing then why it is considfered as the evil to the enviornment?
Without the green house effect, the earth would have an average temprature of -18 degree celcius and be covered in ice.

As it is said that excess of everything is bad, so if we simply understand the concept of green house effect and why it is harmful, then, it can be understand as, consider the atmosphere and earth's surface. Now the sunrays are entering to the earth atmosphere and recahes to the earths surface, in normal scenario, some amount of sunrays are absorbed by the Earth's surface, i.e. 70% and some amount is reflected back to the sky i.e. 30%. If there is normal concentration of the green house gases in the tamosphere then, some of the required heat will be reflected from the atmosphere again to the Earth's surface and hence in this way normal cycle of the green house effect works.

If the concentration of the green house gases increase then the heat more than requred is trapped inside the Earth's atmosphere and keeps on reflecting and as more and more sunrays enter the earth's surface then more and more concentration of heat keeps on increasing the average temprarture of the Earth, and hence it leads to the global warming.

The sky is the never ending beauty, the path to the universe for reaching the heights of infinite explorations for the humanity and mankind. Do not cover them with the curtain of the pollution, just look at it and just have a look at the activities of human beings which are affecting the sky, and covering the way to the universe of infinite beauty, of peace, joy and ecstacy.

"The sky is an infinite movie to me.
I never get tired of looking at what's happening up there."

- K.D. Lang.

# THE FOUR PEST CAMPAIGN OR PROGRAM

What was four pest programme?

The four pest programme is said to be the one of the first actions taken in the "great leap forward" in china from 1958 to 1962. the main aim of this programme was to eliminate some animals like, mouse or other rodents, which are considered harmful for the spread of plague, houseflies, which were considered to spread cholera, mosquetos, which are consideres dangerous as they spread diseases like malaria and dengui, and finally the sparrow, in which Mao Zedong considered it as harmful as it was estimated that one sparrow feeds on atleast 4 pound to 4.5 pound of grains, and also eats fruit.

The main aim of this programme was to make people aware of these animals and dangers they pose to the human beings and Mao and communist government of China forced people to kill these animals in as much bigger number as possible.

Many games and prizes were organized for killing of the sparrows.

Sparrows nests were destroyed, eggs were broken, and chicks were killed. Millions of people organised into groups, and hit noisy pots and pans to prevent sparrows from resting in their nests, with goal of causing them to drop from exhaustion. In addition to these tactics, citizens also resorted to simply shooting the birds down from the sky. These mass attacks depleted the sparrow population, pushing it to near extinction.

If we see the numbers then, it is estimated that, the government and the public were responsible for the deaths of 1.5 billion rats, 1billion sparrows, over 220 million pounds of flies, and over 24 million pounds of mosquetoes. In terms of accomplishing the objective of the four pest campaign, it was a success.

The later effects of the campaign on the ecosystem and economy of the China was very adverse as the poulation of sparrows was reached near to the extinction in China and it also affects the agriculture pattern of the China.

The population of insects and locusts increased and they fed on the crops and fields. This happened due to the decrease in the poulation of sparrows. By 1959, crop production had been reduced by 15%. This decline continued to 70% in 1958. When the famine ended, between 15 and 36 million indivisuals had died due to starvation.

What was this? Did a single species of sparrow effected the economy and agriculture of million of people in China? How?

Well the answer is simple the enviornmnet possess certain patterns according to which the flow of energy in whole the ecosystem and enveiorment keeps on flowing in smooth and equal manner, and if a bit of glitch or disturbance occurs then this pattern is disoriented which leads to the unequal distribution of the energy and certain places or spots in the patterns gets affected in different ways.

This is just an example to understand the importance and role of the tiniest spec of soil present on the Earth, and how each and everything is linked in some manner with each others in manner of tranfer of energy and for their survival on this planet Earth, in a balance of the envionmnet.

It is very easy to undrstand the enviornment and at the same time it is also important to undrstand it and its variouis componets, so that the proper functioning and the balance of the enviornment is maintained that is very important for the survival of the life on this planet Earth and to maintain the beauty of the Earth.

" Smell the sea and feel the sky.
Let your soul and spirit fly."
-Van Morrison.

# WHY WE SHOULD NOT SAVE THE ENVIORNMNET

Now you should be thinking that what are you talking about and what even are you saying? Well I know and it is not even, but it is odd, haha, a bit ironical I know.

The main idea is that we can be successful to, so called, "save the enviornment" from, let us take it as pollution for an instance, in a short term we can be successful to avoid pollution.

In the warmth of, "saving the enviornmnet slogans", we can try the activities for few days to weeks, and for some dedicated ones upto a month, like turning off the tap while brushing, watering plants with cup and bucket, or for some not even watering, as the warmth of saving the water is in their head and heart, and for some not using the car to their work or any other vehicle and try to go on foot or in public transport so that they can contribute towards saving the enviornmnet, and there are many strategies like these we apply to alter or amend our activiteies so that in some ways we can contribute towards saving the envirmnet and our planet Earth, and yes there is trend of another new slogan, "there is no planet- B", and it is very fascinating.

This is the point now where we should try to focus.

It is very simple.

Now in warmth we actually do so many right things or take so many right step with which we acyually contribute to solve the problem of the climate change, which includes, pollution, deforestaion, water crisis and etc. but in warmth we are actually able to do these things upto certain time period, because what is there in our brain is that, "how can I save the planet or I am saving the planet", but when that super hero burden of saving the planet and the warmth keeps on reducing day by day, then the car that was parked for a week take drive almost twicc the distance that some pepke do not even cover in their daily routine of driving their vehicle in one week.

So what is that makes us feel enough when we try so much good for few days and do our best?
Well the answer is simple, you just try to save the thing that is chemically, physically and in all the matters mysterious and huge and complex to human beings and we are not even aware of the processes which are taking place in this planet and this is the thing that we are trying to save.

To be very frank, we are not actually trying to save the planet, we are just saving ourselves. If human beings were immortal then there would be no single human being to stand and raise their voice against the issue of climate change.
Now the important point is that, our way in warmth are good towards the good of enviornment, but the reason is

not appropriate to make a change or reform in the crisis of the global warming and climate change.

What my idea is that if we think just about doing what is right with logics, knowledge, experience and understanding, then we will find that things will become very simple.

There is no need to turn the tap on while brushing, isn't it? There is no need to water the flower with pipes for too long, but if we understand a little then watereirng with bucket and cup will be very great physical work as well as good for enviornment. If you can have a little walk just for your health to the wolrkplace if near you, then why to accelarate the car? Another good option is that why not to have a chat with friends while using the public tranport if the workplace is far from your location?

Don't you think it is simplest of the thing you can do for yoursef but not directly for planet? And if you think you can and if you will ever try this, then it will be surely work for you and enviornmnent in the long run.

The crux is that, insted of thinking to save the envionment, think of doing what is right, and try to question the things that is it relevant that I am doing? Is it the right way of doing this, or is it the thing that is going to help me directly and in some manner, directly or indirectly to the enviornment and our planet Earth?

There are many aspects of being humane when we start dong the things in this manner, then it do not only affects us postively but help us to achieve our ultimate goal.

You will soon find that your good health, is the good health of our planet, Earth.

"Never doubt that a small group
of thoughtful, committed citizens can
change the world; indeed, it is the only thing
that ever has."

-Margaret Mead.

# THE PLANET EARTH

We are trying for past few dcades to minimise the effect of global warming and climate change, and as the most complex organisms on this planet Earth with most advanced neurologiucal setup, we have understand our responsibility towards the other forms of life on this planet Earth.
We can not say that our efforts towards solving the issues of the climate change, global warming and pollution are wasted, instead if no joint decisions by countries around the world at right time was made and by the people contributing whatever they can for the reduction in pollution levels and activities concerned which gives rise to the pollution levels and damage the Earth, then damage to the Earth would be very devastating.
The actions that we took from the past decades had somehow proved that ignorance is not the only cause of isuues like climate change, but lack persistency in out efforts and lack of proper knowledge about the activities concerned with these enviormental issues is the main problem.

With our efforts, persistency towards right actions and knowledge we can somehow find new ways to conquer the situation of the declining condition of the Earth and humanity.

It will be our mere efforts that will somehow lead us to the prosperous, clean and healthy planet.

There are many aspects to this issue of climate change and declining earth's condition, and this book is just a mere set of ideas from my side, which just reflects the condition of the Earth, and shows the extent of the effects of our efforts towards making our enviornment, and Earth, helthy in all aspects, and to rise the feeling of humanity towards the better and proper understanding of ourselves, our actions and our decisions for the betterment of ourselves, the humanity, and our planet Earth.

"It is our collective and indivisual
responsibility...
to preserve and tend to the world in which we live."
-Dalai Lama.

This is not only about one person but the collective efforts of each indivisual on this planet to solve the problem of the declining condiotion of the planet Earth, and to make the Earth green, flourishing and healthy planet for which it is unique in the whole universe, for its amazing diversitry, life and beauty.